The Book of Mindkind

A Philosophy for the New Millennium

William John Cox

Mindkind Publications

www.mindkind.info

Cover Photograph Credit:

National Aeronautics and Space Administration,

European Space Agency,

Garth Illingworth and Dan Magee (University of California, Santa Cruz),

Pascal Oesch (Yale University), Rychard Bouwens (Leiden University),

and the HUDF09 Team.

(Looking into the distance, each point of light in the digital image is an individual galaxy containing billions of stars.)

ISBN 9781519757661

Also by William John Cox

Hello: We Speak the Truth

You're Not Stupid! Get the Truth: A Brief on the Bush Presidency

Mitt Romney and the Mormon Church: Questions

Target Iran: Drawing Red Lines in the Sand

The Holocaust Case: Defeat of Denial

Transforming America: A Voters' Bill of Rights

An Essential History of China: Why it Matters to Americans

Sam: A Political Philosophy

Millennial Math & Physics

PRE-PUBLICATION REVIEWS

"The Book of Mindkind is a tour de force of history. It is much more accessible to the average reader than Stephen B. Hawking's *A Brief History of Time*." ~ Dr. Guy R. McPherson, Professor Emeritus, University of Arizona, *Walking Away from Empire*

"A noble vision for humanity—a philosophy and morality for all to follow." ~ Stan Gibilisco, science writer, Alternative *Energy Demystified*

"Very well put together and readable in one sitting. I couldn't stop reading until I finished it." ~ Rob Kall, editor, *OpEdNews*

"*Mindkind* has an all-encompassing thematic bent that it is very reminiscent of James Burke's wildly successful PBS series *Connections*." ~ Bruce Melton, *Climate Discovery Chronicles: Recent, Relatively Unknown Discoveries About Our Rapidly Changing World* (ClimateDiscovery.com)

"Cox offers an expansive and optimistic account of the history and future of human progress – as well as some bold suggestions on how to keep it going." ~ Matthew Hutson, science writer, *The 7 Laws of Magical Thinking*

"An easy and concise read that is a foundation for replacing the current failed system with a social democracy that benefits all the people." ~ Bev Conover, Editor, *Intrepid Report*

"An interesting philosophical read based on science comprehensible for most readers." ~ Richard John Stapleton, Professor Emeritus of Management, Georgia Southern University, *Business Voyages*

"This brilliant summation of history and noble vision for human-kind's future inspires a fervent wish that *The Book of Mindkind* could become required reading for every student, not only in America, but around the globe." ~ Janet Wise, political novelist of *The Black Silk Road* and *A Midnight Trade* and commentator at *Zeitgeist Change*

"In comprehending the entire text I've had a profound sense that the author has encapsulated an extraordinary amount of data. I have never encountered such a succinct discussion of our universe and our place in it. The text would surprise, inform, and challenge the average lay reader. The book is a compliment to the author's extraordinary intellect and creativity. It is easily comprehensible and well written." ~ Dr. William Tice Vicary, M.D., J.D.

Table of Contents

Prologue.. xi

Part I — Explorations 1

    Time 3

    Earth 9

    Humanity.. 17

    Mind.. 27

    Religion 41

Part II - Discoveries..................................... 51

    Culture 53

    Mindkind 61

    Future.. 73

Epilogue.. 83

    The Soul of Mindkind 85

Sources.. 89

    About Notes 91

    Books 92

    Individuals... 102

DEDICATION

For the Children of Mindkind:

To give wings to your imagination,

Allowing you to soar on the winds of time.

Prologue

Human civilization is at a tipping point. Our population has rapidly expanded during the past 10,000 years of unusually pleasant weather, as we have burned through the stored energy of our planet and moved to occupy its prime real estate.

We must moderate our instinctive drive to consume and reproduce, and we must provide an enriched outlet for the creative energies of our children. Otherwise, our civilization will collapse, a victim of its own success and the vagaries of the climate—our allotted time having expired.

Today, many young people no longer find comfort in the ancient religions, and they distrust existing governments. They are seeking honest answers to the political, social, economic, and environmental questions that threaten their future, and they have little faith in the practices of the past.

The generations who live on Earth today have developed the first crude tools of computerization, which have allowed us to take a few halting steps into space. We are now faced with a stark and simple choice—we either use these marvelous inventions to live in peace and explore the cosmos, or we continue using them for war and ensure our extinction.

There are no other alternatives, and the time for deciding is ticking away.

Part I

EXPLORATIONS

Time

A sense of time seems to be hardwired into life itself. The most ancient creatures were surely aware of the changing tides and the need to migrate with the seasons for nutrition, mating, and birth.

Humans have walked upon the earth for more than 200,000 years, and it appears that marking time was one of the first mental tools we developed. Thirty thousand years ago, an eagle bone was carved with rows of notches, circles, and crescents to represent the phases of the moon and the female reproductive cycle. Six thousand years later, an early sculptor carved the image of Mother Goddess into a rock wall in Southern France. She is depicted as a pregnant woman holding a bison horn cut with 13 notches, designating a lunar year.

The peaceful era of Mother Goddess was replaced by warrior societies, which began to track the annual passage of the sun, in addition to the phases of the moon. The Sumerian civilization, which originated in Iraq between 4500 and 4000 BCE, used a base-60 mathematical system to correlate lunar and solar years and provided us with our 60-second minute, 60-minute hour, 24-hour day, 12-month year, and 360-degree circle.

At about the same time, the Egyptians relied on the predictable flooding of the Nile River and the annual ascension of Sirius, the brightest star in the night sky, to calculate an accurate 365¼-day calendar.

Julius Caesar's affair with Cleopatra in the First Century BCE produced more than a great love story; he also adopted the Egyptian calendar year for the Roman Empire. The Julian calendar required that the month of February have 28 days, except that every fourth year was a "leap year" in which February received an extra day.

Following the collapse of the Roman Empire and the subsequent religious suppression of knowledge during the Dark and Middle Ages, the intellectual advances in science and mathematics of the Renaissance were required before the Julian calendar could be improved upon.

The astronomical calculations of Nicolaus Copernicus in the Fifteenth Century provided the scientific basis for disproving the Catholic Church's geocentric dogma—which placed the earth at the center of the universe—and laid the foundation for the modern calendar. Nonetheless, fearful of Church authorities, Copernicus delayed publication of his work until he was on his deathbed.

Since the Julian calendar year was eleven minutes too long, its use had caused a ten-day problem in the celebration of Easter by the mid Sixteenth Century. On February 24, 1582, Pope Gregory XIII issued a decree continuing Julius Caesar's leap year system, "except for years that are exactly divisible by 100," and with the further exception that "the centurial years that are exactly divisible by 400 are still leap years." Thus, 2000 remained a leap year, while 2100 will not be since it cannot be evenly divided by 400.

The Gregorian reformation established the more accurate Copernican year of 365.2425 days, and it skipped 10 calendar days to restore the vernal equinox on March 21.

Although opposition to the lost days slowed adoption of the Gregorian calendar by England (and the American colonies) until 1752, this calendar is the one that still hangs on walls around the world.

Modern timekeeping resulted from the efforts of mariners and mapmakers to determine longitude, which requires the ability to calculate exactly how many minutes of difference exist between any location on the globe and the Universal Prime Meridian in Greenwich, England. The first accurate marine chronometer was developed by John Harrison, who was rewarded for his invention in 1773.

The advent of computers, global positioning satellites, space travel, cellular phones, instantaneous international finance, and the Internet created the need for a more exacting measure of time. Even a slight variation of time can make a huge difference in space navigation and the synchronization of computers.

Rather than celestial movement, Coordinated Universal Time is now measured by the element cesium, whose atoms oscillate more than nine billion times each second. In the United States, time is determined by a collection of 50 atomic clocks feeding information into a bank of computers at the Naval Observatory in Washington, D.C. The combined system keeps time accurate to less than a billionth of a second per day.

With the recent discovery of Earth-like planets around other stars, we are now contemplating travel to these distant star systems. How long will the journey take?

A speed of about 25,000 miles per hour (mph) is required to escape the earth's gravity. NASA's New Horizon space craft has achieved the fastest speed yet of 36,000 mph (58,000 km/h) in its exploratory trip to Pluto.

Since the distance to Proxima Centauri, the nearest star to Earth, is almost 25 trillion miles (40 trillion kilometers), the voyage would take almost 80 thousand years at the New Horizon speed. If, however, we can imagine it possible to achieve the speed of light (186,282 miles per second, or almost 300,000 km/s), we could make the journey in just four-and-a-quarter years. Even at the speed of light, a trip to Andromeda, the closest major galaxy beyond the Milky Way, would take two-and-a-half-million years.

The wave of previously unimaginable discoveries in just the last century demonstrates there is vastly more we do not know than we currently understand. Travel through space in the future may simply require that we spin into an adjacent dimension and reappear in the solar system of Proxima Centauri, in the Andromeda galaxy, or on the other side of the earth, in which case the voyage could not and would not be measured by time or distance.

On one hand, greater mastery of the ability to divide time into ever more discrete elements will be necessary to coordinate the computerized machines required to accelerate us through space and time. On the other hand, use of those machines to skip over the great distances involved in space travel will make time increasingly irrelevant, since we will either be here or there and not in between.

Although no serious cosmologist currently entertains the likelihood of time travel, once we learn to travel timelessly through adjacent dimensions, a passage to the past or future may be discovered. Just because time travel is currently beyond our scientific comprehension does not mean it is forever impossible.

We can only imagine such things. They are presently unknown, but they are not necessarily unknowable.

For now, time remains a valuable tool to mark our progress from the past into the future. It establishes the period of our residency on this lovely blue and white planet, orbited by a large silver moon, as we slowly circle around a warm yellow star embraced in the arms of an elegant spiral galaxy, we call the Milky Way.

Earth

Compiled about twenty-six hundred years ago in Israel-Palestine, the *Book of Genesis* (1:1) informs us that "In the beginning God created the heavens and the earth." The *Rig Veda* (10.129.1-7), however, reflecting an even older religious tradition in India asks, "Who really knows, and who can swear, how creation came, when or where! Even gods came after creation's day."

Based on his literal reading of the *Holy Bible*, the scholarly Archbishop Ussher of the Church of Ireland deduced in 1654 that the first day of creation commenced about 6,000 years ago, precisely, at nightfall on the evening before Sunday, October 23, 4004 BCE.

Although some religious fundamentalists still cling to this late date for creation, most people try to look beyond cultural folklore to understand the physical planet we live on, how it came into being and where it is heading. There are, however, as many differing scientific theories of origin as there are creation myths.

Currently, the most accepted scientific theory of cosmology is that the entire universe was instantaneously created and suddenly inflated from a subatomic spark of pure energy in a "big bang" about 13.8 billion years ago and has been smoothly expanding ever since. Expansion, however, is being seriously challenged by the emerging theory of a static universe of plasma[1] shaped by electromagnetic forces. The following working draft of a cosmological conjecture offers an alternative to the Standard Cosmological Model.

> *We theorize the existence of an eternally negative cosmos, occupied throughout by an infinite, static, physical universe of plasma, whose electro-magnetic filaments generate cosmic dust from massive electrical currents of free electrons and ions. Surrounded by spiraling magnetic fields, pinched filaments of electricity drag the surrounding plasma into dynamos creating the proto-matter of positive, galactic mass having lifespans that allow the stars to produce occasional planetary gardens of life and mind—naturally, without initial creation or ultimate judgment.*

The star we call Sun, or Sol was born in the Milky Way galaxy approximately 4.6 billion years ago. There are about 100 billion stars circling in

---

[1] A plasma results from the heating of a gas such as hydrogen and consists of unbound negatively charged electrons and positively charged ions (protons).

the galaxy, and each orbit of the sun takes about 200 million Earth years. The sun is a medium-sized star, and the material left over from its creation gravitationally organized itself into the present planets, asteroids, and a surrounding shell of comets. The surface temperature of the sun is around 10,000 degrees, with its atmospheric corona increasing up to 300 times.

Along with Mercury, Venus, and Mars, Earth is a spherical rock. Beyond Mars is the asteroid belt, followed by the gaseous planets of Jupiter, Saturn, Uranus, and Neptune. Pluto, first thought to be a planet, is now relegated to the status of other similar objects that orbit beyond the natural planets.

Although we perceive the earth as being solid, it is in fact a molten mass which is only cool at the surface where it is exposed to the cold vacuum of space. The crust is blanketed by a dense gaseous atmosphere that rapidly grows thinner and colder with higher altitude. In reverse, the earth's heat increases with depth, until its nickel-iron core reaches almost 10,000 degrees Fahrenheit, with the outer core reaching almost 14,000 degrees Fahrenheit.

The molten interior of the earth helps to keep us warm. It also creates electrical currents that swirl outward as a magnetic field—which surrounds and protects us from solar radiation and produces the beautiful auroras at the poles.

Relatively, the solid crust of the earth we live on is very thin, much like the shell of a bird's egg, and it would be equally smooth, if reduced to the same size. Given its dense atmosphere, its ability to retain water, and its ideal distance from the sun to gently warm its surface, Earth is currently a hospitable place for life.

A significant, and perhaps rare, event took place about 4.5 billion years ago. That was the creation of the moon—which drives the ocean tides and helps to produce the weather and geological processes that make life possible.

A cataclysmic collision occurred between the earth and a planetary object about the size of Mars. The combined momentum produced so much heat that the crusts of both were melted. The earth absorbed some of the object's mass, including its metallic core; however, the remainder, along with some of the earth's crust, splashed out and formed a ring around the earth.

Over time, the ring coalesced into the moon, which ultimately surrendered its rotational energy to the earth. Locked into a stable orbit, the moon always presents the same face to the earth, allowing the two of them to embrace each other in a slow waltz around the sun every year.

The collision increased the spin of the earth, providing us our brief 24-hour day, unlike the one-year day of Venus. It also resulted in a slight tilt to the earth's axis, which causes our varying seasons and further enhances the chance of life.

The reconstituted earth continued to be bombarded by asteroids, comets, and meteorites carrying water, oxygen, carbon dioxide, and organic compounds allowing the planet to become a liquid oasis, washed to and fro by moon-driven tides.

This then is the world we live upon. Magnifying the crust beneath our feet, we can see within each grain of sand the various chemical atoms it is composed of. Looking more closely, we find the sand to be alive with movement, as electrons flash around the nuclei of atoms, and the atoms continually bounce off each other.

Peering inside each individual atom, we find that, compared to the infinitesimal size of the nucleus and the orbiting electrons, each contains vast amounts of empty space. In addition, atoms are not like marbles, which can be tightly packed together. Atoms are mostly nothing, and they magnetically repel each other—creating space around themselves.

While we may feel we are standing on solid ground, we are mostly standing on nothing, and the human bodies we occupy are also primarily composed of empty space. If we could shrink down to the size of an electron, we might "fall through the cracks" beneath us. No matter how solid our bodies and our surroundings appear to be, all positive mass is alive with constant movement within the empty negative space it occupies.

On the physiological level, Mother Earth, including us humans and all her other animal and plant life forms, is a collective living organism. Everything interacts together to form a self-regulating system that allows for the survival of life on Earth.

Beginning as early as the Neolithic Age, and certainly by commencement of the Industrial Revolution, permanent geological evidence of human activity on Earth has been laid down. This era has been named the Anthropocene (Greek, *anthropo* - "human" and *cene* - "new"). What it will be known for is undetermined—although it appears we may be contributing to and driving the sixth mass extinction of life on our mother planet.

Whether or not we humans remain a part of the earthly equation remains to be seen. We may have the means to commit suicide, but we do not have the power to destroy the garden in which we live. At least, not yet.

Humanity

The earth we live upon appears to be the same from day to day; however, over the eons, the hard surface has migrated over a viscous interior, reforming itself, over and over, into continually changing continents, oceans, and climates.

The land has been repeatedly covered with dense forests of plants and trees, which have been swallowed up and submerged under the surface to form coal. Over the eons, living organisms in the oceans died, settled to the bottom, became buried under rock, and were ultimately transformed by heat and pressure into petroleum.

For a variety of reasons including shifts in the earth's orbit around the sun, the migrating tilt of its axis, movement of its crust, and concentrations of greenhouse gases, the weather conditions on Earth can vary over time. Sometimes it is too hot, sometimes it is too cold, and only occasionally is it just right.

We are most familiar with "ice ages" in which glaciers slowly flow over land areas in the higher latitudes before retreating; however, there have been periods when the earth's surface was completely covered with ice. The last time was about 650 million years ago when, from outer space, Earth would have looked like a gigantic snowball.

There also have been times when the surface of the earth resembled a burning hell. A 20-degree increase in temperature caused worldwide fires 250 million years ago that incinerated 95 percent of life.

Another fiery catastrophe occurred 65 million years ago when an asteroid the size of Mount Everest struck the ocean off the Yucatan Peninsula of Mexico. The asteroid was pulverized—the blazing hot dust rose into the atmosphere, and an intense heat consumed vegetation around the world.

The atmospheric dust and ash blocked the life-giving rays of the sun, and the earth was plunged into a deep freeze. A sulfuric acid rain finally cleared the dust from the atmosphere, which in turn created a "greenhouse" phase. The global thermometer was reversed, and Earth suffered high temperatures for the next half-million years.

The dinosaurs, who had dominated the earth for millions of years, failed to survive; however, tiny mammals, who had evolved following an earlier die-off, were able to thrive by feasting on the carrion and detritus that remained. One of them was our direct ancestor.

In our family tree that has flourished since that time, we can identify a progenitor primate in Africa about five million years ago from whom we are descended, along with our cousins, the apes, chimpanzees, and bonobos.

Approximately two million years ago another member of our family tree known as *Homo erectus* arose in Africa. It wandered as far abroad as Indonesia and Asia, before becoming extinct around 140,000 years ago. In 1891, a 430,000-year-old mussel shell was found in a riverbank on the island of Java near a *Homo erectus* fossilized skullcap. What is unique about the shell is a zigzag engraving, which was precisely incised with a sharp tool, such as a shark tooth. This is the earliest known symbolic or artistic expression.

About a hundred thousand years ago, our branch consisted of three sprigs of proto humans. There was the Neanderthal group in Europe and around the Mediterranean Sea, a Denisovan group in Indonesia and mainland Asia, and a group in Africa that survived the other two.

Genetic testing has established the probability that all of us *Homo sapiens* are related to a single woman and her relatives who lived in Africa about 140,000 years ago. As her descendents migrated around the world, her genes became mixed with those of the other two groups, but she lives on in each of us.

The human hybrid resulted in a magnificent species with a brain three times larger than other primates. We became bi-pedal and developed the speed and endurance to run down prey and to travel over long distances foraging for food. The better we ate, the better we thought, and improved thinking further increased the food supply, the quality of life, and the chances of survival.

A genetic mutation may also have driven our migration, as we continually explored beyond the safety and comfort of our homes. A variation in the gene that causes the brain to provide rewards for learning and exploration is more often found in migratory societies. An increase in the genetic variation has been identified in those groups that traveled the greatest distance out of Africa, and individuals who bear the mutation tend to be stronger and better nourished than those who remain by the hearth.

What makes us uniquely human? Is it our large brains, our skillful hands, our predisposition to travel, our language ability, or all of these?

We have had big brains throughout human history, and we've been making fire and tools for a very long time. More than a million years ago, in the time of *Homo erectus,* the basic hand ax was already standardized throughout Africa, Europe, and much of Asia. Having the ability to first imagine what a finished ax should look like, before it was knapped from a cobble of stone, indicates the presence of abstract thought.

Evidence of symbolic language has been found among artifacts in Germany, which were dated between 250,000 and 350,000 years ago. Among them was an elephant tibia clearly marked with seven and fourteen straight lines.

Humans were using tools, exploring, and expanding our horizons from the beginning; however, it was language that propelled us so quickly to where we are today. While the making of stone tools can be physically demonstrated, verbal language allows for the description of the fruit and wildlife that exists in a far distant river valley, the phases of the moon, the passage of the seasons, and the navigational constellations in the sky.

From the moment we created verbal language to better teach what we learned to others, especially our children, we have been able to move beyond the limitations of instinct, to acquire and improve upon knowledge—and to teach the tool of learning itself and the value of language and exploration to each new generation. Language enables us to cooperate with each other more effectively in achieving a more orderly and productive society.

Verbal language also helped forge the strong social bonds that have allowed human babies to slowly develop physically and mentally during the longest childhood of any species. Nurtured by all members of a tribe or village, children were provided the opportunity to absorb the breadth of knowledge and experience available in their culture.

Happy and well-nourished children more easily develop the social skills, empathy, and impulse controls necessary to become successful adults. An innate sense of fairness and a willingness to help others is a strong survival trait reinforced in childhood. Over time, altruism, at least on the local level, became intrinsic in all human cultures.

We developed a deep-seated sense of morality based on the need to share the hunt and the fruits of gathering. We came to deplore repulsive behaviors and evolved a basic system of justice. Nonconformists were shunned, and serious offenders were banished from the group—which was equivalent to a death sentence.

Humans learned the value of caring for the elderly who, although they could no longer hunt or gather, could teach their skills, and share their wisdom and experience with the children and young people of the group.

Archaeologists have found evidence in ancient burials of individuals who were able to live to an advanced age despite serious disabilities. Compassion was developed for the sick and the lame, even though they may have consumed more than they could contribute. Scientists have discovered that helping others stimulates activity in the area of the brain involved in rewards and pleasure.

Deeply felt emotions became a characteristic of humans. Other creatures also experience feelings—there is pleasure in the act of procreation, birds mate for life, and elephants and chimpanzees mourn the loss of family members. Humans, however, are the only species that exhibit a full range of emotions.

We experience real joy. We laugh out loud, we make music, we sing, and we dance. Humans embrace romantic love. Our pulse races when we think about the object of our affection. We write love stories, poetry, and songs. We become temporarily insane.

We suffer deep sorrow. We sob uncontrollably—we become depressed, and we commit suicide. We mourn the death of a loved one. For tens of thousands of years, we have been placing flowers in and on the graves of the deceased, and, like elephants, we return to the burials over and over.

We also have a conscience. We flush and feel a sense of shame when our thoughts and deeds fail to meet the cultural expectations of our society or the ethical standards we have established for ourselves.

Our nearest relatives on the evolutionary tree are apes, chimpanzees, and bonobos—with whom we share more than 95 percent of our genes. It is, however, with the bonobos that we find more of the emotional characteristics that make us human.

While apes and chimpanzees can act out violently against each other and other species, the bonobos, who evolved in a geographic area free of competition with the other two, are more apt to "make love, not war."

Bonobo groups are dominated by females. They frequently engage in promiscuous sex, easily make friends, and they peacefully resolve disputes within the group without violence.

Along with the apes, chimpanzees, and the bonobos, we are all descended from the same proto ape which lived in Africa. The aggression of apes and chimpanzees may have resulted from their forced competition; however, the peaceful bonobo behavior could be more representative of our original shared ancestor. Perhaps, the positive human characteristics we attribute to social conditioning have a genetic basis.

Much of the deception, hatred, and violence we experience today is intolerant brainstem behavior, resulting in a disease which we must overcome or cure if we are to fully mature into our essentially peaceful and cooperative nature—that which makes us human.

Just like finding cures for physical diseases, we must study both the pathology and physiology of the mental and emotional processes that give rise to deception, hatred, and violence. To do that we have to achieve an understanding of the human brain and the mind it produces.

Mind

The name of our human species, *Homo sapiens,* results from us being a member of the primate family *Hominidae*, the only surviving member of the genus *Homo*, and from the Latin word, *sapiens,* which means wise or intelligent.

All animals on Earth are believed to have descended from a tiny half-billion-year-old creature like a segmented tube worm. This first animal had a simple digestive tract and a nervous system extending along its length, consisting of groups of nerve cells linked together, with a larger bulb, or brain at one end. Most basically, the nervous system compelled the animal to seek and consume food, reproduce, and avoid danger.

The bulb of the ancient chain of nerve cells has evolved into the large and complex human brain, which sits on top of our spinal cords, through which nerves reach out to every element of our bodies. The brains of humans, along with all vertebrate and most invertebrate animals, are divided into two halves that are, essentially, mirror images of each other.

We are the only species on Earth equipped with a mind that incorporates our entire being, expanding beyond our brain to encompass the entire sensory perception of our body and all that surrounds it—so far as our mind can reach. One mind compelled a body to write these words, and another causes a body to read and interpret the words. The gap between the two events is essentially unlimited by time or distance.

Since strongly felt emotions can cause physiological responses within the chest, consciousness was once associated with the heart; however, Hippocrates, the ancient Greek physician, wrote that perceptions, emotions, knowledge, and wisdom come from the brain, which exercises power over the body.

As a human embryo develops, its nerve cells organize themselves into billions of *neurons*, each of which sprouts transmitters called *axons* and receptors named *dendrites*. The axons and dendrites approach each other, without touching, at trillions of junctions, or gaps, known as *synapses*. The seemingly random growth of axons, as they migrate throughout an embryonic brain, is a genetic ballet choreographed to bring them to a precise place for each to effectively transmit and receive signals to and from other neurons.

Most basically, a neuron transmits an electric signal along the length of its axon until it reaches a synapse between it and the dendrite of another neuron, whereupon a chemical is released which crosses the gap to stimulate yet another electrical impulse. A reverse flow sometimes occurs, or, in some cases, a direct electrical connection may be made. In either case, the transmission process is very rapid, or almost instantaneous—think how quickly the hand recoils after touching a hot stove.

Maintaining the brain's extensive electrical system requires an inordinate amount of energy, with the brain consuming almost one-quarter of the body's metabolic output. The electrical power resulting from this consumption of energy generates a field that can be measured from outside the skull.

We share most of our genes with other animals, especially other primates, and we have 99.99 percent of our genes in common with all other humans. From the moment of birth, however, these similarities diverge, as our personal life experiences create a vastly different array of unique synapses within our brain. Known as the "connectome," the brain's neural circuitry stores our memories, creates our minds, and defines our being.

Except for most nerve cells, all other human cells go through a birth and death cycle at different rates that essentially gives us an entirely new body every decade. The billions of nerve cells, however, particularly those of the cerebral cortex, remain intact throughout life. This phenomenon not only preserves our essential lifetime memories, but it is the reason the frightened child and awkward adolescent—who lives on within each of us—influences our emotions and actions throughout our lives. It is why the elderly can still revel in the exuberance of youth—mentally, if not physically.

At each stage of its evolution, the brain kept what worked and added what was needed, piling ever-higher mental processes on top of the ancient brain which governed eating, reproduction, and fight or flight. Primarily, it is the cerebral cortex that provides the definition and means for the mind to come alive and to talk to itself.

The human brain has grown to be three times larger than that of our nearest relative, the chimpanzee. Magnetic resonance imaging reveals that the expansion of human brains has resulted in a vast increase in the association areas connecting sensory and motor functions. Much like the Internet, these areas develop as organized chaos—which provides the framework for complex minds and individual personalities.

There may be as many as 100 billion neurons in the brain, each communicating with 10,000 other neurons. These form 100 trillion connections, or switches, all of which are either "on" or "off" in the manner of modern computers. In the aggregate, the synapses of a single human brain can store a trillion gigabytes of information and may provide more mathematical possibilities than there are atoms in the known universe.

The brain's activity can be compared to a rushing and surging river, with the brain structure being like the riverbanks and sandbars carved into the earth's crust. Were the river to be dammed and the water suddenly released, it would mostly follow the same sinuous path to the ocean, altering the surface along the way.

Our magnificent connectome provides the ability to listen to music and to later replay it in our memory, to learn to read and write music, to play instruments, to sing and to join with others in an orchestra or chorus, and to dance. We can see the world unfold around us as we pass by, and we can later visualize and describe what we experienced. We can cook, using a wide variety of ingredients and spices, smell and taste the differences in recipes, share our food with others and later remember what we were talking about as we were eating. Years later, our ability to recall allows us to see, hear, and smell these events and to feel the emotions they produced once again.

Thus far, the best efforts by scientists to accurately duplicate brain function involve the connections of perhaps a dozen of the billions of nerve cell networks in a single brain. An IBM supercomputer simulation of approximately 10 billion neurons ran 1,500 times slower than the human brain and required several megawatts of electrical power. Full speed would consume as much electricity as that which powers both San Francisco and New York City.

While scientists have been able to locate and map some of the brain's functions, much remains mysterious, including consciousness, memory, learning, intelligence, conscience, emotions, dreams, language, communication, cooperation, creation, imitation, truth, deception, violence, sanity, and the aura of mind.

Although the two sides of our brains are physically similar, they experience and influence our lives very differently. Neither dominates, and the efforts of each are essential in our ongoing struggle to survive in a competitive and threatening environment.

During our early evolution, in the time before language, the right hemisphere directed our existence. Much like the other animals in the forest or on the plain, we used our right brain to perceive the physical environment around us in finding food and surviving danger.

Our right brain is suspicious, and it intuitively connects patterns from our sensory inputs to provide a mental picture of our immediate surroundings. The right is immersed in the "here and now," including the contentment, fear, and pain it experiences.

With the development of language, we achieved a powerful tool to make sense of our world and to ease our passage through it. The job of managing language has been assigned to the left brain of all but a very small minority of left-handed individuals.

If our right brain suspects, it is our left brain that confirms or denies the suspicions and tells us what it decides. Do we trust or distrust what we are being told? The left-sided detective figures things out by examining the details and deducing the truth, while the right-sided skeptic relies on nonverbal clues to intuitively identify falsity.

The right brain may provide leaps of insight about art, music, and mathematics, but it is the left brain that patiently guides the paintbrush, writes the musical notes, or proves the formulas. The left brain reads these words, but it is the right that imagines the pictures they create. Or the left creates and uses language to describe what the right side sees.

The right brain films our existence, but the left brain edits and organizes the sequences into a comprehensible video that provides us with a continuum of time. It compares the past with the present and predicts the future.

The left side generates our self-image, telling us if we are looking good or acting stupid. The left is the judge, juror, and executioner of our conscience. It is the voice we hear in our head every hour of every day, except when we sleep.

We experience the dream world in the right side, as the left silently watches. Dreams help to move our short-term memories into long-term storage and to rehearse strategies to confront the challenges of the coming day.

The left interprets our dreams and can actively direct them when we intentionally engage in "lucid dreaming," which permits us to take our problems to bed and awaken with solutions.

Except for vision, our senses are hardwired to the opposite sides of our bodies. The fingers on the right side of the keyboard are controlled by the left brain, and the sound waves of music entering the left ear are directed to the right side of the brain. Vision is a little more complicated in that the left side of the visual perception of both eyes is directed to the right half of the brain, and *vice versa*, the right side of our binocular vision is conducted to the left half of our brain.

The tie that binds the two halves together and which transmits the sensory perceptions from one to the other is a flattened half-donut-shaped sheaf of 200 million nerve fibers known as the *corpus callosum*. Acting as a switchboard to connect areas with similar functions and the mirror-image points of each side of the cortex, the corpus callosum processes billions of bits of information each second.

Thus integrated, our brain is the seat of our consciousness, our self-awareness, and our relationship to the world we inhabit. Humans are not, however, the only animal capable of feelings and perception.

Those of us who live with domesticated animals, such as dogs and cats, have no need of scientific experiments to conclude that they are not only conscious, but that they are quite adept at manipulating their environments, including their owners. Dogs can be observed to demonstrate shame, joy, exuberance, courage, and loyalty and to engage in active dreaming. To live with a domestic cat is to experience being the subject of a ruling monarch.

Self-awareness by animals has been demonstrated by the "mirror test," which involves placing a colored dot on their foreheads and seeing whether the animals attempt to touch or remove the dot when observing themselves in a mirror. Our dog and cat friends fail the test; however, the great apes, elephants, dolphins, and orcas demonstrate self-perception. Even European Magpies and trained pigeons have been reported to identify themselves in the mirror. Human children first exhibit the ability when they are about 18 months old.

Once we are aware of our consciousness, we can also identify subconscious processes, including instinct, which are not a part of our active mental focus, but which play a valuable role in our existence.

Our ability to engage in multi-task thinking is demonstrated as we carry on a conversation with someone we encounter, while we try to remember their name and where we know them from, try to figure out what they are really saying, and wonder why they are wearing such a ridiculous outfit. The same thing occurs when we communicate in a foreign language and simultaneously translate meaning and context.

Encompassing consciousness and self-awareness is the concept of mind, which extends as a virtual aura beyond our physical body as far as it is experienced, perceived, or has influence. Here, the mystery of existence extends to the nature of the mind, and we begin to wade into the depths of the unfathomable— as there is even less known about our minds than there is about the brains that produce them.

With the development of our minds, we humans evolved into something different from our animal ancestors and living cousins. We are not just wise and intelligent apes; we are an entirely different being that uses our minds to adapt the earthly environment to our needs, as we explore the limits of our planet and create marvelous things along the way.

We have become our minds, as we think about the process of thinking, and we evaluate the consequences of our thinking and emotions. We not only have the ability to learn, but we have the capacity to think about how to learn and to teach ourselves how to think and behave better. The product of all of this is our evolved facility to imagine something in our minds, to create it with our hands, or to direct its completion by others. For good, bad, or indifferent, we imagine something in our minds, and we act upon it.

One does not have to be a scientist, engineer, artist, or author to understand and appreciate the magnificence of our creations. Raise your eyes from these written words to the book or computer screen that contain them. Examine the paper and binding of the book, or the monitor and computer that produces the words, and contemplate the creative processes that went into their invention and production. Look around the room in which you sit at the objects that surround you, gaze out the window into your neighborhood and at other buildings, the passing automobiles, and the airplanes that fly overhead. Take a moment to appreciate the magnificent culture we live it. Click on Google Earth, take a virtual trip around the world, zoom in on the Great Wall of China, the Pyramids, and modern cities, or search the Internet for beautiful satellite photographs of our universe.

Who are we? We are creators!

From the moment we used our imagination to shape hand axes to more effectively obtain and process food, the foundation was laid for the creative culture in which we now live. Everything along the way, from art, music, and books, to computers, has been an extension of that process—as we individually invent and create useful and interesting things, and we collectively imitate the works of others. As Einstein believed, "The secret to creativity *is* imitation."

Our brains are the coordinators of our bodies, which have become vehicles for our minds. While we can still look in a mirror and see a male or female, young or old, beautiful, or ugly body, what makes us who we really are is the molding of our minds by nurturing, emotions, family, community, education, culture, religion, philosophy, and politics.

We are our minds, and what we know, and use is no longer contained within our individual brains. The fingers that operate the keyboard also have instant access to computerized dictionaries, thesauri, encyclopedias, and (thankfully) spell check. References include more than the hundreds of books collected on the surrounding shelves—our knowledge base also incorporates the public libraries and the millions of documents and images that can be instantly accessed on the Internet. Much of the collection of human history, discovery, and creation is now only a keystroke away.

To cope with the enormous amount of information required to survive and thrive in our modern human society, we are born with large brains, experience long childhoods, and receive structured educations. Yet, even with all this, no one human can wrap her or his mind around all that is known. We not only depend on and make use of external information—our minds have become an integral part of the larger whole.

While we each remain uniquely individual, our minds are merged with those of all others with whom we coexist in a collective consciousness. Thus united, we will solve the problems that confront us and jointly experience our destiny. The survival of our species depends on this collaboration and our ability to achieve and sustain it.

Language, particularly the written word, is the foundation upon which our worldwide civilization is constructed. Universal access to its store of knowledge is required if we are to effectively use it to imagine and create the means to break free of the bonds of Earth, and to share our lives and creations with like-minded relatives throughout the living universe.

Even with all we have individually learned and collectively know, the truth remains elusive. There are differences of opinion about everything written here, and corporate, economic, social, and political pressures cause our information to be intentionally manipulated and distorted in ways that pervert the truth.

Just because most of us believe something is true, does not mean it is beyond dispute. There are no absolute truths in science and mathematics, as all propositions exist only until such time as they can be effectively disproven.

The search for truth has continued throughout human existence, and things which could not be easily explained or understood often became a matter of superstition or religion. For many, the only truths are those revealed by their religion, and others, hearing a voice in their head, believe they are receiving direct communications from God.

Religion

Religion has been a fellow traveler from the beginning of human consciousness, and it continues to provide comfort to people who fear that which is beyond their knowledge and experience to understand. Having faith or a belief in something that cannot be proven or disproven must fulfill basic human needs, otherwise religion would not exist.

Early in our human development, religion evolved to help us cope with the struggle to survive and to explain the mysteries of procreation, birth, life, and death.

We think, imagine, and dream from the moment we are born, and it is difficult to conceive of a dark, empty, and silent lack of existence once we die. It is easier to believe we will go on thinking and experiencing emotions and perceptions in a happier place.

As caring and empathetic individuals, we don't want to surrender our relationship with someone we love. Permanent separation is painful, and we want to maintain the spiritual presence of loved ones who have passed on. They continue to exist in our minds. We can smell them, and we can hear their words. We can touch their tears, and we thrill to the sound of their laughter. We sense their lingering presence, and we need to believe they are still with us. We cannot accept they cease to exist. Even if there is no afterlife, a belief in its existence provides comfort to those who mourn, and for those who fear death.

The stress of life drives us to believe in something greater or more powerful than our own selves. Religion comforts us and makes us feel better. Its practice produces rewards in the chemistry of our brains. We are happier and less depressed.

Religion provides guidelines to encourage and enforce morality, which is beneficial to society. Having a common belief system allows for group cohesion and, collectively, the family or tribe is more successful.

Before we learned the facts revealed by science, we relied on religion to explain the apparent movement of the moon, sun, and planets. Matters such as migration, hunting, and planting came to depend on our ability to make predictions about the seasons. What did it matter if everyone believed that God reversed the transit of the sun when it got too cold in the winter and provided the rejuvenation of spring? The important thing was that seeds were planted at the right time—if there was to be the miracle of harvest in the autumn.

Early religion was associated with healing and—with the discovery of mind-altering and medicinal plants and alcohol—shamans and healers provided physical, mental, and emotional support and escape from the drudgery of earning a living.

Throughout history, spiritual worship has provided much of the art, music, song, and dance that has served the social needs of groups. Religion has allowed artists, musicians, and architects to express their talents and exhibit their creations.

For tens of thousands of years, we worshipped life itself, and the images we dig out of our earliest settlements are those of healthy, pregnant women. We peacefully coexisted with nature, and our Mother Goddess presided over a nurturing society based on the feminine attributes of empathy and collaboration. What is not found is evidence of organized destruction, burning, or war.

Well into the more complex agricultural societies of the Neolithic Period in the Sixth and Seventh Millenniums BCE, there is widespread evidence of the worship of Mother Goddess. In western Turkey, archaeologists have found numerous shrines and cult rooms in which female goddesses are prominently displayed, including one sitting on a throne flanked by two lions. Women may have tamed the wild animals, but men were soon to take the credit.

Perhaps it was the discovery of bronze and the ability to make deadly weapons which facilitated the revolution in which the husband and sons of Mother Goddess seized control of her nurturing society and turned it into the horror of violence and perpetual war—one that has continued until the present.

The first warrior nations of the Middle East depicted their masculine gods sitting on the throne as though *they* had tamed the lions. There were multiple gods, and they fought continually among themselves for power and dominance.

Today, Jews, Christians, and Muslims believe in the masculine and judgmental God found in the *Old Testament* of the *Holy Bible*. The Canaanite God was known as El, and *Exodus* (6:3) has God explaining that He revealed Himself to Abraham, Isaac, and Jacob as El, instead of Yahweh. In the Hebrew language, the word, *Elohim* is an alternative name for God, and it has both singular and plural meanings.

Deuteronomy (32:8) reveals that just before his death, Moses spoke about the plurality of gods: "He fixed the bounds of the peoples according to the number of the sons of God." While Yahweh became the God of the Hebrews, He was but one of the sons of El. (Revised Standard Version).

El's wife was named Asherah, and some Iron Age inscriptions also identify her as the wife of Yahweh. Women continued to worship Asherah until the reforms of King Josiah in the Seventh Century BCE. Josiah presided over a rewriting of the *Bible* to weave a continuous story about the people of Israel, and he established Yahweh as their one and only God.

Josiah celebrated a renewal of the covenant with God, and he ordered the destruction of all altars dedicated to El and Asherah, including those built by King Solomon. Archeological excavations in Jerusalem have uncovered hundreds of figurines of the Mother Goddess destroyed by Josiah.

Everything associated with the worship of Mother Goddess was eliminated. Ordinary women—concerned with matters such as menstruation, conception, pregnancy, childbirth, and the nurturing of children—no longer had a place to go for compassion and comfort.

Although contemporary Judaism considers the Hebrew God to have both male and female aspects, the primary role of Jewish women, particularly among the Orthodox, is to be wives and mothers, and they are discouraged from religious pursuits.

The original Christianity founded upon the historical teachings of Jesus was revolutionary in that women played a leadership role in the Christian Church for hundreds of years. The *Gnostic Gospels* honor the Divine Mother as Wisdom, or Sophia, and have Jesus speaking of "my Mother, the Holy Spirit." These *Gospels* also reveal that Jesus' "companion," Mary Magdalene—whom he loved most of all—had the greatest understanding of his teachings. Mary was the most honored of Jesus' disciples; however, the Catholic Church slandered her for centuries as a prostitute until 1969 when Pope Paul VI cleared her name and reputation.

The Pharisee Saul, who persecuted the first Christians, converted, and became Paul. He began to create a theology at odds with that of James the Just, the biological brother of Jesus. Historically, James served as the leader of the original church of Jesus— known as *The Way* or *The Poor*—for 26 years until his own murder by stoning in 62 CE. His beliefs are found in *The Book of James* (2:17), where he taught that "faith by itself, if it has no works, is dead."

Paul not only revised Christian theology to allow justification by "faith apart from works of the law," (*Romans* 3:28) but he also reversed Jesus' position on the role of women. In his *First Letter to Timothy*, Paul instructed: "Let a woman learn in quietness with all submissiveness. I permit no woman to teach or to have authority over men; she is to keep silent." (2:11-12)

Religions, and the male-dominated bureaucracies that have evolved to govern them, have continued to serve the warrior societies in the subjugation of women.

While the Catholic Church has come to venerate the Virgin Mary as the Mother of God over the past 1,700 years, it has effectively eliminated the participation of women as priests and bishops. Moreover, by prohibiting both birth control and abortion, the Church has denied the freedom of choice to women as to whether they are able to bear the burden of pregnancy, childbirth, and the nurturing of children. Women continue to have the greatest responsibility for the raising of children in every society and culture.

The role of women in Islam—the second largest world religion—has been equally repressive. It is the right of Muslim men to command women (except to defy Allah), and it is the duty of women to obey. The main purpose of marriage in Islam is for women to bear children, and most forms of birth control are forbidden to them.

The third largest religion is Hinduism. With a billion followers, primarily in India, it is the oldest living religious tradition. Hinduism commenced with the collection of ancient sayings in the *Rig Veda* and ultimately organized the sacred Hindu scripture known as the *Bhagavad Gītā*.

Hinduism is complex, inclusive of differing traditions worshipping a variety of deities, all based on the ancient Vedic religion. Most Hindus believe in repeated reincarnations, until freedom is achieved through salvation based on one's practices and "karma." The role of Hindu women is dependent on the tradition they follow, with some more restrictive than others. All traditions, however, recognize that

God has both female and male aspects, and there are both male and female deities.

Buddhism is the fastest growing religion, with slightly fewer than one billion adherents practicing the teachings of the Buddha, who lived in India around 485 BCE. Encouraged to engage in ethical conduct, Buddhists believe that beings experience a succession of lifetimes and various life forms, as they either perform good or bad actions that spring from mental intent constituting one's karma. The ultimate goal is to achieve enlightenment and to be reborn into the pure abodes of the higher heavens. The Buddha recognized that women can realize the truth as much as men, and there is a general equality between the sexes in the religion.

Confucianism, the widespread system of ethics and conduct based on the teachings of Confucius (551-479 BCE), was particularly obnoxious to the place of women in society. Women were required to obey their fathers, husbands, and even their sons. A recent revival of Confucianism by the Chinese communist leadership emphasizes its respect for authority and downplays sexual discrimination.

Religious fundamentalism, a growing and disturbing world-wide trend, aggressively proselytizes, institutionalizes intolerance of other faiths, and often incites violence in the suppression of contrary views. Militant Christianity in the United States, jihadist

Islam in the Middle East, expansionist Judaism in Israel-Palestine, Hindu assassins of secular intellectuals in India, and even radical Buddhism in Myanmar, ignore the peaceful and progressive tenets of each religion in favor of repressive ideologies of hatred, intolerance, and narrow-mindedness toward others. Joining the fundamentalist movement, some atheists have developed a rigid and dogmatic lack of respect and intolerance of all religions.

Today, more than half of all people, practicing as many as 20 different major religions, believe in God. The numbers, however, are rapidly declining, particularly among young people. Even among people of faith, many "don't know what happens" after death, and more than one-quarter do not believe in a heaven or hell.

A loss of faith in established religions has contributed to the rise of humanism as an ethical and philosophical alternative to traditional doctrines. Humanists believe in a quest for knowledge, the preservation of human rights, and compassion for others.

Many of the wars that have been fought since the evolution of warrior societies can be attributed to religious differences, greed, or power. Indeed, history is normally taught as a chronicle of cultures, their religions, their governments, and their wars. Given, however, the population, economic, environmental, and militarization crises facing humanity today, it seems more instructive and beneficial to consider what we, collectively, are doing right, rather than what we are doing wrong.

It appears to be true that we need to believe in something—perhaps, we should have faith in ourselves, our accomplishments, and our own creations.

Part II

DISCOVERIES

Culture

Humans are quite simply the most marvelous species that has ever evolved on the earth. We have adapted Earth's environment to our needs, and we have multiplied to fill every habitable niche of its surface.

We have created a magnificent and cooperative worldwide culture based on our ability to work together in solving complicated problems. As a group, we are more intelligent than the smartest individual among us, and our collective common sense is the foundation of human wisdom.

We usually communicate the truth and demonstrate respect and civility in our interactions. Were you to travel to every country, every city, and every village and enter every home, every apartment, and every hut where humans live, you would find parents who love and care for their children and who wish for them a better and safer existence. Everywhere, people are helping others in need and communicating their discoveries and inventions in making life easier for all.

The essence of humanity is that we mostly tell each other the truth, and the truth we tell is that we care for one another.

Coming to fruition in just the last century, human inventiveness has lifted the heavy burden of labor from the backs of women and workers in most countries. A vast expansion of knowledge has accompanied the laborsaving machines and has resulted in an ever-increasing rise in human intelligence.

Physiologically, the larger knowledge base requires our brains to work harder, and the exercise increases our brain function. We are smarter than we were a century ago, but there is so very much to learn—we struggle to absorb it, yet our children simply take it for granted.

It is fortunate the new generations are more intelligent and knowledgeable than the older folks, for the tasks they will face are formidable. The four horsemen of the modern Apocalypse are not Conquest, War, Famine, and Death; they are Population, Economy, Environment, and Militarization.

The first of these, the population explosion, is the easiest to solve. Simply give women equal opportunity and guilt-free control over their own bodies. Provided with knowledge, economic freedom, and access to safe and effective methods of birth control, women will only bear the number of children they can afford to safely raise. The world birth rate will drop dramatically.

Economically, we have engaged in the exchange of materials, goods, and services throughout our existence. Archaeological evidence of trade has been identified at very early sites in which items such as red ochre, obsidian, perforated seashells, and semiprecious stones are found far from their place of origin.

A person skilled in making tools from flint could trade the product of his efforts for meat and vegetables obtained using tools made by others, and tribes could exchange materials that are abundant near their villages for scarce commodities from other areas. Language—first verbal, then written—facilitated economic trade.

Written communication using incised counting tokens was developed 11,000 years ago to allow a purchaser in one area to know just how many oxen, goats, or measures of grain were entrusted to an agent by a distant merchant. Subsequently, written symbols were directly impressed into small sheets of wet clay allowing the creation of dried tablets which could convey and document commercial transactions, government functions, and cultural stories.

Different forms of written communication evolved around the world, and with the invention of the printing press, readily translatable books allowed for the rapid diffusion of knowledge into every language.

In just the last few decades, computers and smartphones remotely connected to the Internet by Wi-Fi or transmitted by fiber-optic cables and satellites allow for the instantaneous transmission of both personal and economic data around the world. We can now travel to any place on Earth within a day or so, cellular phone service is available in most settled areas, and global positioning satellites allow us to know exactly where we are.

None of this would have been possible without the creation of large commercial enterprises capable of organizing finance, research, materials, and labor to construct the machines and infrastructure required to make it all happen.

Corporate organization may be necessary to build great things, but corporations must be carefully controlled and regulated, otherwise they will take over. Corporations are like robots. They have extraordinary potential power—and a lack of conscience—and since their goal is to earn the greatest return on their investment of capital, they are dangerous to the environment and to the freedom of individuals.

The global power of corporations has grown exponentially as they have come to command natural resources, manufacturing, and finance. Wealth is not only concentrated in the advanced nations at the expense of developing countries, but it is becoming increasing hoarded in the vaults of a wealthy elite at the expense of workers and small business owners, resulting in the destruction of the middle class. At the same time, corporate exploitation and predation are destroying our environment.

There must be an equality between labor and capital; however, neither corporations, nor labor unions can be allowed to run the government that necessarily regulates them. We can no more allow corporations and labor unions to possess the rights guaranteed to individuals than we can entrust the prison keys to the convicts.

A system of sensible regulation and fair taxation must be based on reason rather than greed, and it must result in an economic structure that provides rewards for most people, and which discourages inequality of opportunity. We must trust the inherent goodness and common sense of ordinary people and provide them with the knowledge and means to exercise their individual freedoms—and to formulate the policies of their governments more directly.

We have seen that the earth naturally experiences broad swings in its climate and that more often than not, it can be an inhospitable place for human existence. The development of our civilization has been encouraged by unusually pleasant weather during the last 10,000 years.

The natural environmental order is being disrupted by human (and corporate) activity—which is, at least, exacerbating the problem. The drive for profits and immediate gratification is delaying and obstructing efforts to survive in the future during extreme climatic conditions. Corporate exploitation and aggressive marketing of rapidly diminishing fossil fuels not only suppresses efforts to secure alternative energy, such as space solar power, but it also pollutes fresh water supplies by hydraulic fracking, mining dirty coal, and exploiting filthy tar sands.

There is incontrovertible evidence that carbon dioxide concentrations and global temperatures are higher today than they have been in thousands of years, and that they are likely to continue rising until they meet and exceed levels that haven't been experienced since before the last ice age.

Unrestrained population expansion and unregulated corporate schemes are accelerating global warming, and the window of opportunity for the survival of our species is rapidly closing.

Creating a system of alternative energy and ensuring the fresh air, clean water, and nutrition necessary for human survival will not be cheap or easy. In fact, it will be difficult and expensive. Humans have the inventiveness to come up with solutions and the ability and experience to organize and apply the fix, but where will the money come from to pay for it?

Quite simply, we must end the senseless wars that have continued uninterrupted for hundreds and thousands of years. In just the last century, the unchecked power of militarism has diverted massive and incalculable financial resources to the wasteful purchase of the destructive machines of war resulting in the deaths of more than 100 million people.

The existing military expenditures by nations—worldwide—are more than sufficient to underwrite the availability of nutrition, education, and health care for every child on Earth and to organize the resulting human capital into productive endeavors essential to human survival.

There is no alternative. The worldwide warrior society not only consumes natural and financial resources, but it is also eating at the very soul of humanity. We have evolved a reluctance to kill; however, by encouraging and training our young people to murder one another—virtually through computer games, personally with firearms and remotely by satellites, drones, and rockets—we are destroying everything that has brought us to this point. At long last, after millions of years of struggle and wandering, we are on the verge of achieving the ability to fly from our nest!

If we continue to glorify violence and the military, the only consequence will be the total elimination of our personal freedoms and another world war. There will be no victor.

Which brings us to the ultimate questions. What are we? Are we destroyers, or are we creators? Which do we want to be?

Will we continue our exploration beyond Earth and throughout the cosmos, or will we self-destruct?

Mindkind

Half of all adults and three-quarters of young people believe it is likely there is intelligent life on other planets, and more than one-third of all adults believe Earth has been visited by extraterrestrials. These beliefs are deep-seated and have endured throughout human history.

Genesis (6:4) reveals that once upon a time "the sons of God came into the daughters of men, and they bore children to them." The offspring of the sons of God became known as the Nephilim.

In the *Book of Jubilees* (5-1) we are told:

"And when the children of men began to multiply on the surface of the earth and daughters were born to them, . . . the angels of the LORD saw . . . they were good to look at. And they took wives for themselves from all of those whom they chose. And they bore children for them; and they were the giants."

For in his days, the angels of the LORD descended upon Earth—those who are named The Watchers—that they should instruct the children of men, that they should do judgment and uprightness upon Earth."

According to the Jewish Talmud, "God flies through 18,000 worlds," and the Zohar speaks of seven earths inhabited by intelligent creatures.

The official astronomer of the Catholic Church—that once convicted Galileo of heresy for saying the earth was not the center of the universe—has acknowledged there could be intelligent life in outer space.

The *Noble Qur'an* frequently mentions the possibility of extraterrestrial life, such as "He is the LORD of all the Worlds" (1:2), and "among His signs is the creation of the heavens and the earth, and the living creatures that He has scattered through them." (42:29)

Since the first modern incident in 1947, there have been thousands of reported sightings of flying saucers and other unidentified flying objects (UFOs), and hundreds of photographs and videos have been obtained. The United States government investigated many of these reports; however, efforts were primarily devoted to debunking, rather than verifying contact. Even so, almost one-quarter of the reports could not be explained.

In November 2011, the White House stated, "The U.S. government has no evidence that any life exists outside our planet, or that an extraterrestrial presence has contacted or engaged any member of the human race." The statement went on to say, however, that the "odds are pretty high" that there may be life on other planets, but "the odds of us making contact with any of them—especially any intelligent ones—are extremely small, given the distances involved."

Astronomers have instituted a search for planets outside our solar system that might support life, resulting in the launch of the Kepler Space Telescope in 2009. An analysis of data from the telescope reveals that Earth-like planets may exist around one in five Sun-like stars in the Milky Way galaxy. If true, there may be as many as 25 billion habitable planets just in our galactic neighborhood. Nearly 2,000 individual exoplanets have been identified, some of which are Earth-like and orbiting in the "habitable zone" where liquid water could pool on their surfaces.

We cannot be alone in the universe. Eternity is far too long, and the universe is much too vast for the small planet we live upon to be the only place where intelligent beings have evolved. In terms of probabilities, it is highly improbable that life only exists on Earth. Our failure to identify extraterrestrial life is a measure of our limitations rather than the likelihood of its existence.

Only a few centuries have passed since we believed Earth was the center of the universe, and a hundred years ago most astronomers thought the Milky Way galaxy constituted the entire universe.

Now, we are on the threshold of accepting that even our perceivable universe is but a tiny part of something larger, and that eternity is but a moment in a timeless infinity.

To the extent we think, our intellect compels us to seriously consider these propositions: Earth is not the only planet in the universe capable of sustaining life; the spark of life is a natural product of chemical processes; life has flared up at locations other than Earth; and intelligence is the ultimate expression of sustained life.

As to the nature and origin of life, the only thing we know for certain is that we are a part of life as it presently exists on Earth. We are less sure of when, where, and how that life began; however, science is zeroing in on the answers.

Scientists have found proof of early life in rocks that can be reliably dated to 3.8 billion years ago. Life may have come into being as early as four billion years ago—if it originated in deep ocean hydrothermal vents instead of on the surface.

We are now sure organic molecules occur naturally in interstellar dust clouds and likely existed in the sun's protoplanetary disk, even before Earth and the other planets were formed. There is also a good chance organic molecules hitchhiked to Earth on asteroids and comets.

Solid evidence continues to accumulate about how organic chemicals evolved into self-replicating molecules and protocells, and ultimately into RNA- and DNA-based life. Amino acids necessary for metabolism and the building of proteins may have been created by natural energy sources, such as lightning, ultraviolet irradiation, or the heat of meteor impacts. One exciting discovery resulted from the laboratory recreation of the ocean's iron-rich catalytic environment as it was four billion years ago. Researchers have documented spontaneous chemical reactions much like those observed in living organisms.

While there is little doubt that chemistry-to-life evolution has taken place on Earth, we cannot yet conclusively prove life has arisen at other locations. Nonetheless, there is increasing circumstantial evidence it has.

The possibility of extraterrestrial life is supported by the discovery of bizarre life forms on Earth at extraordinarily harsh places, such as deep in basaltic rock totally cutoff from photosynthesis, or in boiling sulfuric hot springs. Giant mouthless tube worms and blind shrimp absorb chemical nutrients at deep ocean vents, and microbes thrive in the slime and darkness of deep caves. These findings suggest life is possible on planets with different environments than Earth.

Our neighboring planet Mars offers a strong case for having its own home-grown life forms. When telescopes were first focused on Mars, some observers believed they could see a network of canals constructed by intelligent beings. While this theory has been disproven, what has been established is that Mars undoubtedly had an abundance of flowing water in the ancient past.

In 2004, the National Aeronautics and Space Administration (NASA) landed two self-propelled rovers on opposite sides of the Mars surface to conduct scientific surveys. One of the rovers, Opportunity, found evidence of the mineral hematite, which is normally formed in water. Spirit uncovered rocks rich in chemicals formed when Mars was warmer and wetter than it is today. Among these chemicals was silica, which is created in hot springs or hot steam vents.

Silica, scientifically known as silicon dioxide and commonly called sand, is a compound of the element silicon. As the most abundant mineral on the Earth's surface, silica is found throughout the human body, particularly in the skin, tendons, ligaments, bones, and teeth.

A more sophisticated robotic rover, Curiosity, landed in 2012 to expand the search for evidence of microbial life on Mars. Curiosity has identified an ancient lakebed, which may have provided a home for microbes. More specifically, Curiosity has measured spikes in the organic (carbon and hydrogen) methane in the atmosphere and detected different organic molecules in the surface rocks it has drilled into.

In September 2015, NASA was able to confirm that water continues to flow on the surface of Mars. An imaging spectrometer on an orbiting spacecraft documented downhill flows of water—which varied with the seasons.

Opportunity and Curiosity continue to patrol the surface of Mars looking for evidence of life, and there are plans for another spacecraft to visit the planet in the future to collect rocks and return them to Earth for more detailed examination.

It is not necessary to wait, however, as rocks from Mars have already arrived on Earth. When a planet is struck by an asteroid of sufficient size and speed, it can cause material from the surface to splash out into space and escape from the planet. That orphan material can then be gravitationally captured by another planet and fall to its surface as a meteorite. Scientific examination of these rocks may provide evidence of life on the first planet.

One such 1.3-billion-year-old Mars meteorite was discovered in Egypt in 1911. When examined in 2006, the meteorite was found to contain a series of microscopic tunnels like those caused by terrestrial bacteria. These findings were confirmed by examination of another Mars meteorite of the same age found in Antarctica in 2000. Expelled from Mars during the last 10,000 years, the Antarctica meteorite was confirmed to be like the Egyptian meteorite in containing fossilized evidence of bacteriological activity. Scientists cannot presently rule out the possibility the tunnels were formed by nonliving processes, and the jury is still out.

Even if we assume there are other planets capable of sustaining life and that life has in fact arisen on those planets, we are still left to wonder if such life has achieved intelligence. Although there have been numerous sightings of UFOs, we have yet to see an extraterrestrial interviewed on the evening news. How confident can we be that intelligence is the natural consequence of life?

We will undoubtedly debate the issue until extraterrestrial life forms choose to communicate with us; in the meantime, we can use our own intelligence to arrive at some logical probabilities. Homo sapiens was not the first human species to make and use stone tools and to create art and symbolic language, and we are not the only species presently on Earth that has achieved self awareness. Others such as our closest cousins, the chimpanzees, recognize themselves in a mirror and can demonstrate the intelligence of human toddlers.

If we continue along our self-destructive path and succeed in killing ourselves off, is there any real question that someday—millions of years in the future—the chimpanzees or some other life form will achieve a level of intelligence equal to or in advance of our own? If that could occur here on Earth, it has surely taken place at other times and locations in the universe where life has become established.

Assuming long-term survival, what is the ultimate manifestation of intelligence, as it evolves over time? Does it become more militaristic and warlike, conquering and destroying all it encounters? Or does it become more cooperative and peaceful? Which attribute contributes the most to sustaining life and longevity? Which is the most productive, creation or destruction?

Most likely, the successive evolutionary stages of chemistry, life, intelligence, and tranquility are as constant throughout the universe as the periodic table of chemical elements. If this is true, is it not also true that the highest stage, intelligence, or mind, has the duty to serve as a guardian for all life, at every stage of development and wherever it may be found?

Simple logic tells us there is intelligent life beyond Earth and, if so, that any being sufficiently advanced to visit Earth can do so only because its energies are directed toward peaceful exploration, rather than conquest.

Imagine the excitement when a new life-sustaining planet is discovered, with the opportunity to witness the birth and development of another intelligent species and to watch, enjoy, and appreciate its creations.

Throughout an unlimited universe and during all of eternity, everything we create here on Earth is unique. While sciences such as chemistry, mathematics, and physics may be immutable, our art, music, and architecture have never been created before. Especially, the solutions and strategies we invent to solve our economic, environmental, political, and social problems here may be studied and used elsewhere.

From what we know today with certainty and what we can surmise with confidence, it is safe to believe we have been watched over for millions of years, as we slowly pecked through our shell, and we will be lovingly looked after until we learn to fly from our nest.

As there is but peace throughout the universe, we will be grounded here until such time as we, ourselves, overcome and cure the diseases of deception, hatred, and violence which infect us, individually and collectively.

We are not quarantined. It is just that we will never achieve the ability to acquire sufficient knowledge, wisdom, and power to travel to any significant place in the universe, into adjacent dimensions, or forward and backward in time, until *every child on Earth*, irrespective of race, religion, culture, or social condition, has equal access to nutrition, health care, and education.

That which is presently unknown is far too vast for it to be discovered by the sheltered and unassisted progeny of the intellectual, political, and financial elite. It will take the combined effort of all our children to comprehend and penetrate the multi-dimensional veil that shrouds life beyond Earth.

If we fail to grow up and we are stillborn in our own waste, millions of years may again pass, as the ruins of our self-destruction are scoured by the winds and rains of time, until another intelligent being looks up, notes the phases of the moon, marks the solstices of the sun, sights the planets moving among the stars, and learns to fly.

For surely, the rare blue water planets of warm yellow stars, nursed by large silver moons in the outer arms of elegant spiral galaxies, are too precious to be wasted. These are the nests where the eggs of creation are found, where all that is beautiful is born, where we nervously stand with our fledgling wings spread wide, and where the Children of Mindkind are brought forth.

Future

From what we have learned thus far, we have the inherent ability to evolve to meet new challenges. The only question is whether we have the collective strength of character and flexibility of mind to endure. If we believe strongly enough in ourselves, and if we are prepared to think for ourselves, we will do what is required to allow our children to survive and thrive in the new millennium.

Let us imagine we can visit the not-so-distant future and observe what our progeny have been able to accomplish—once they have cured themselves of the intolerant brainstem diseases of deception, hatred, and violence and have ensured all children have equal access to nutrition, health care, and education.

Our governments have come to care for and nurture the people who elect them, knowledge is widespread, women participate equally, and the individual rights of everyone are protected and defended, irrespective of race or status.

Rather than having to choose among politicians and the platforms they propose, the people more directly make their own policies through referenda, and they choose representatives they believe will best implement their policies.

Paid election holidays honor the voters, as they celebrate the most sacred sacrament of their political religion. Informed voters demonstrate their power over their governments, as they thoughtfully answer the policy questions on their paper ballots and carefully write in the names of the candidates they choose.

Corporations, labor unions, and other fictitious legal entities no longer enjoy the constitutional rights of individuals. They are carefully regulated and reasonably taxed to ensure they fairly share the burden of their existence, and they are not allowed to become so powerful as to threaten the rights and safety of individuals or the sanctity of self-government.

National governments are entirely supported by a slight toll tax on every financial transaction, including currency speculation, interbank loans, trade in stocks and bonds, and the payment for all goods and services throughout the economy.

The substantial tax revenues raised by the fair and simple toll tax provide complete funding for education at the local and state level through college. Tuition is free for all students through community college, through a bachelor's degree for young people who contribute a year of valuable public service upon attaining adulthood, and through a master's degree for those who contribute two years.

Proceeds of the toll tax are also adequate to completely pay for national health, dental, optical, and mental health care for everyone, irrespective of wealth or income. Medical clinics have been established in all educational facilities serving their students and residents of the immediate neighborhoods, and on-site health care is provided in all businesses—once they employ enough workers.

The cost of providing health care and worker's compensation insurance has been lifted from all employers, resulting in a rise in both productivity and profits.

Individuals who opt out of the national health system and obtain their own health care are allowed a deduction on their annual toll tax return for the *per capita* value of national health care. In practice, because of the very low taxes paid by individuals and the very high quality of national health care, very few people choose private insurance.

Safe and effective methods of birth control are freely available for all women, who have the unrestricted personal choice whether they will bear children. Irrespective of their decisions, women receive the full support of their families, communities, and governments.

With the heavy cost of public health care and education lifted from municipal and state governments, general welfare assistance is largely provided on a local basis where needs can be more accurately, fairly, and economically accessed and administered.

The size of national governments has been substantially reduced, as their mission has been redirected from the enforcement of complex regulations to the establishment of binding legal presumptions and minimum damages. These procedural devices reduce the cost of doing business and the burden of litigation. They are relied on by aggrieved individuals and businesses when they present their complaints to the courts or privately arbitrate their disputes.

National governments have established their own independent banks, which issue the national currency and loan money for government operations. The saving of interest formerly paid to private banks has greatly reduced the cost of government.

Government banks have become the depositories for solvent national retirement systems, which operate in addition to the safety net of social security insurance. Voluntarily contributed by workers and their employers, and guaranteed by the government, retirement funds are primarily invested in small businesses and the construction and maintenance of national, state, and local infrastructures.

Increased investment and reduced costs have reliably improved the ability of small businesses to compete in world markets, resulting in economic stability—internationally. The economy is providing jobs to everyone who wants to work, and a balance between labor and capital has been achieved.

All businesses, including large corporations, have come to recognize it is to their advantage to have a well-paid, healthy, rested, and happy workforce and have joined with organized labor to support improvements in basic working conditions. The standard now includes a sustaining minimum wage, paid sick and maternity leave, four weeks of annual paid vacation, and a four-day workweek, allowing a three-day weekend or an extra day off in the middle of the week.

The number of countries continues to increase, as large artificial nations peacefully resolve themselves into more logical self-governing constitutional entities.

The threat of militarization has been defeated, and the international trade in armaments has been eliminated. Governments maintain only very small, but effective defensive forces, which are backed up by volunteer national guards and militias.

All countries have renounced war against other societies as an instrument of national policy. Instead, specifically named individuals, who are proven to pose a danger to the safety and security of their own people and to those of other nations, are now declared to be outlaws, and legislative warrants are issued for their physical arrest. Disputes between governments are arbitrated in the World Court of Justice, rather than on the battlefield. Freed from most conflicts, governments concentrate on solving their own problems, rather than meddling in the affairs of others.

The booming international economy is powered by the energy derived from extensive space-solar collectors placed in gyrosynchronous equatorial orbits (GEO) by a consortium of world governments. The GEO system is primarily dedicated to providing free energy by electrical induction in the surfaces of all major highways and rail systems for inexpensive transportation around the world.

The remaining electrical grid system has come to rely on the widespread use of wind and wave generators, and solar collectors—which have resulted in a substantial reduction in the use of fossil fuels and nuclear reactors.

With independence from the need to use fossil fuels for energy, governments have prohibited fracking, the mining of dirty coal, and the exploitation of tar sands as unjustifiable threats to the fragile water supply and shared environment. In addition, with the containment of corporate power, aggressive enforcement of clean water standards has facilitated widespread improvements in the quality of water. Concurrent with these changes, the private ownership of water systems has been prohibited, guaranteeing the continued delivery of affordable, clean drinking water around the world.

Altogether, these changes have resulted in a major reduction in individual and collective stress, and a consequential drop in crime and violence. An initiative to voluntarily reduce the ownership of personal firearms has resulted in the construction of magnificent monuments to the curtailment of violence in front of courthouses and government buildings in every country. These memorials to the victims of violence were built by welding guns, knives, and other weapons into creative and impressive modern sculptures, where streaks of rust have replaced the stains of blood.

The worldwide War on Drugs ended with the decriminalization and reasonable regulation of the personal possession and use of all drugs. With the loss of their markets and enormous profits, the drug cartels and criminal gangs have been disbanded, and the level of associated violence has plummeted. The personal use of drugs has shown an equal decline, as education and treatment options have enabled and empowered individuals to make rational decisions—rather than to be influenced by cultural glorification or being intentionally addicted by drug dealers.

Social and medical improvements in the care and support of the mentally ill minimize the threat of harm they pose to themselves and others.

The private operation of all correctional facilities has been prohibited, and the number of prisons and prisoners has been considerably reduced. The criminal justice system has been effectively reoriented from punishment to rehabilitation. With increased educational and employment opportunities, most people convicted of crimes—particularly youthful offenders—benefit from supervised probation rather than incarceration.

Perhaps most importantly, we find that the energy of young people has been redirected from gangs, drugs, and nihilism towards games, competitions, and creative endeavors, such as art, music, dance, drama, and the design and invention of an endless stream of new and improved computerized devices and software.

Or our visit to the future may be a very sad and disappointing experience.

We may find that nothing has changed, and there has been no improvement in the quality of individual lives, governments, the economy, or the environment. The never-ending wars and suppression of human freedoms continue, and the chances are that humanity will not survive. It will just be a matter of time—as the collapse quickens.

While this dismal view of the future may be distressing to us personally, it won't make a whole lot of difference in the larger sense.

Our demise will be mourned by those who have patiently and lovingly watched over us since the blossoming of our consciousness; however, the Garden of Earth will not be destroyed. Although damaged, her rivers will once again run clean to the oceans within just a few hundred years, the air will eventually clarify, and life will go on. We just won't be around to enjoy it.

Perhaps another million years or so will pass until another intelligent being evolves on Earth and learns to fly. The last few artifacts of our civilization may be found and another child of Mindkind will wonder about us, and ask who and why?

The 140,000 years of human existence is but a moment in time to Mindkind, and even if we fail to fly from our nest, our creative contribution to the universal culture has been phenomenal. We have much to be proud of, some to be ashamed of, and more than we can presently imagine to hope for.

We still have a way to go and, as we stand here at the tipping point of our destiny, we must recognize our inherent goodness, unite together, draw upon our collective resources, and focus our energies on the common objective. The creed of Mindkind requires that we, the Children of Mindkind on Earth, make it on our own and that we do it together.

Epilogue

The Soul of Mindkind

Sequencing of the human DNA has proven the extent of our relationship to other primates and to each other. The complexity and collaboration of the effort provides hope for the ultimate mapping and replication of brain functions and the mind itself, including our collective consciousness.

Based on our biological nervous system, cutting-edge research is now allowing computers to mimic the human brain as they automate and self-adjust their programming to perform assigned tasks. Moving beyond massive brute-force programming, third millennial computers will learn to cleverly see, listen, evaluate, compensate, and communicate with ever increasing speed, precision, and elegance.

The Human Brain Project of the European Union is trying to completely simulate the human brain, and the United States government is funding the Brain Initiative—a $4.5 billion effort to map the brain. As ambitious as these projects are, they are only tentative steps toward a comprehensive theory of the human brain and the mind it produces.

Much like pressing a button on a key as we approach our parked automobile and unlocking its doors, and just as our cell phones communicate with others by bouncing signals off distant receivers, we may find the power of our minds extends beyond the physical limits we presently find comprehensible.

The time may come when our bodies become expendable and we leave them behind—as our minds travel to places and times presently unimaginable, in an equally fantastic and instantaneous manner.

Our nascent ability to map the brain's chemical and electrical paths and energy fields offers clues for solving the mysteries of the mind itself. Searching beyond the limitations of our bodily existence may reveal a path to a practical understanding of our "soul."

One of the most intriguing areas of computer research involves the application of quantum physics to facilitate parallel computations. These studies have contributed to a theory that consciousness is the product of quantum mechanics inside the microtubules located within brain cells. This proposition suggests our soul may survive during near-death experiences and following actual death—as the quantum information cannot be destroyed and must be conserved. The theory has been supported by the discovery of quantum vibrations within these microtubules and by the revival of full brain function in individuals whose bodies have stopped functioning for extended periods due to extreme cold.

Once we establish the nature and extent of our living mind, we may find there is a rational basis for the age-old question of life after death. If the soul, or the aura of an individual's mind, independently survives the physical body, there must be a focus for its tenuous energy—a nexus where its material force can be realized. It may be that the soul only survives when the individual who bore the mantle of its corporeal existence is thought of in the mind of another.

Perhaps our personal heaven and hell exists whenever and wherever we are remembered with either admiration and respect, or with disdain and revulsion. In either case, our surviving spirit may have no choice but to enjoy the love, or endure the hatred earned during the period of our bodily existence. The way we choose to live our lives and to exercise our free will may not only affect those who share our living space, but our eternal pleasure or suffering as well.

Only time will tell whether these last few thoughts have validity or whether there is time enough remaining for validation.

For now, time continues to unwind moment by moment. Our collective intellect struggles against the brutality of ignorance and superstition that seeks to destroy it, and we must fight and win the battle ourselves.

Victory depends upon the valor and wisdom of those who follow us in life and who will boldly lead us into the future—The Children of Mindkind on Earth.

Sources

About Notes

Research material has been accumulated by the author in notebooks and file folders for more than 30 years, and certain chapters are based, in part, on two earlier publications, *Mindkind: Math & Physics for the New Millennium* and *Time Travel to Ancient Math and Physics.*

Due to the condensed nature of the book, direct footnotes and references were not used in the interest of brevity and word flow—as many if not most sentences would require multiple footnotes. Following, as best as can be reconstructed, is a summary of published sources and a list of individuals, whose valuable work influenced and contributed to this effort. Most will hopefully recognize and approve of the use of their work. Sincere apologizes are offered for any unintentional slights in attribution, or for the failure of recollection and documentation of other contributions—the origins of which have been lost to time and memory.

In law, attorneys often use the Latin phrase *sine qua non* (without which there is nothing) to refer to something that is indispensible or essential. Without access to the vast body of knowledge represented by the following, this little book could not have been conceived or written.

Books

Alexander, John B., *UFOs: Myths, Conspiracies, and Realities* (Thomas Dunne Books, 2011).

American Museum of Natural History, and Michael J. Novacek, *The Biodiversity Crisis: Losing What Counts*, (The New Press, 2001).

Armstrong, Karen, *Muhammad: A Prophet for Our Times,* (HarperOne, 2007).

---, *Buddha,* (Penguin Books, 2004).

---, *Islam: A Short History,* (Modern Library, 2002).

---, *In the Beginning: A New Interpretation of Genesis*, (Ballantine Books, 1997).

Bamberger, Bernard J., *The Story of Judaism*, (Schocken, 1964).

Barrett, Justin L., *Why Would Anyone Believe in God?*, (AltaMira Press, 2004).

Behie, Alison M., Ed., and Marc F. Oxenham, *Taxonomic Tapestries: The Threads of Evolutionary, Behavioural and Conservation Research*, (Anu Press, 2015).

Berger, Lee R., and Brett Hilton-Barber, *In the Footsteps of Eve: The Mystery of Human Origins*, (National Geographic, 2000).

Bering, Jesse, *The God Instinct: The Psychology of Souls, Destiny and the Meaning of Life*, (Nicholas Brealey Publishing, 2010).

Berns, Gregory, *Iconoclast: A Neuroscientist Reveals How to Think Differently*, (Harvard Business Review Press, 2010).

Bjorklund, David F., *Children's Thinking: Cognitive Development and Individual Differences*, (Cengage Learning, 2011).

Bloom, Paul, *Descartes Baby: How the Science of Child Development Explains What Makes Us Human,* (Basic Books, 2005).

Boleyn-Fitzgerald, Miriam, *Pictures of the Mind: What the New Neuroscience Tells Us About Who We Are*, (FT Press, 2010).

Boyer, Pascal, *Religion Explained: The Evolutionary Origins of Religious Thought,* (Basic Books, 2007).

Bronowski, Jacob, and Richard Dawkins, *The Ascent of Man*, (BBC Books, 2013).

Burrows, Millar, *The Dead Sea Scrolls*, (Secker & Warburg, 1956).

Carroll, Michael P., *The Cult of the Virgin Mary*, (Princeton University Press, 1992)

Cavalli-Sforza, Luigi Luca, and Francesco Cavalli-Sforza, *The Great Human Diasporas: The History of Diversity and Evolution*, (Perseus Books, 1996).

Chalmers, David J., *The Character of Consciousness (Philosophy of Mind),* (Oxford University Press, 2010).

---, *The Conscious Mind: In Search of a Fundamental Theory*, (Oxford University Press, 1996).

Ceram, C.W., *Gods, Graves & Scholars: The Story of Archaeology*, (Alfred A. Knopf, 1967).

Charlesworth, James H., Ed., *The Old Testament Pseudepigrapha*, (Hendrickson Publishers, 2010).

Coomaraswamy, Anada, *Buddha and the Gospel of Buddhism*, (University Books, 1969).

Dawkins, Richard, *The God Delusion*, (Mariner Books, 2008).

Deamer, David, *First Life: Discovering the Connections Between Stars, Cells, and How Life Began*, (University of California Press, 2012).

Dennett, Daniel C., *Kinds of Minds: Toward an Understanding of Consciousness*, (Basic Books, 1996).

de Waal, Frans B.M., *The Bonobo and the Atheist: In Search of Humanism Among the Primates*, (W.W. Norton & Company, 2014).

---, *The Age of Empathy: Nature's Lessons for a Kinder Society*, (Crown, 2009.

Diamond, Jared, *The World Until Yesterday: What Can We Learn From Traditional Societies?*, (Penquin Books, 2013).

Drake, Frank, and Dava Sobel, *Is Anyone Out There?*, (Delta, 1994).

Duncan, David Ewing, *Calendar: Humanity's Epic Struggle to Determine a True and Accurate Year,* (Harper Perennial, 1999). (Of particular value in the chapter on Time.)

Eisenman, Robert, *James the Brother of Jesus: The Key to Unlocking the Secrets of Early Christianity and the Dead Sea Scrolls,* (Penguin Books, 1998).

Eisler, Riane, *The Chalice & the Blade: Our History, Our Future,* (HarperOne, 1988).

Finkelstein, Israel, and Neil Asher Silberman, *The Bible Unearthed: Archaeology's New Vision of Ancient Israel and the Origin of Its Sacred Texts,* (Touchstone, 2002).

Flynn, James R., *Are We Getting Smarter?: Rising IQ in the Twenty-First Century,* (Cambridge University Press, 2012).

Frankfurt, Harry G., *On Truth,* (Knopf, 2006).

Freke, Timothy, and Peter Gandy, *Jesus and the Lost Goddess: The Secret Teachings of the Original Christians,* (Harmony, 2002).

Friedman, Richard Elliott, *Who Wrote the Bible?,* (HarperOne, 1997).

Gascoigne, Bamber, and Christina Gascoigne, *The Christians,* (Morrow, 1977).

Gilbert, Adrian G., and Maurice M. Cotterell, *The Mayan Prophecies,* (Element, 1999).

Gimbutas, Marija, and Joan Marler, *The Civilization of the Goddess: The World of Old Europe*, (HarperSanFrancisco, 1991).

Glimcher, Paul W., and Ernst Fehr, *Neuroeconomics, Decision Making and the Brain,* (Academic Press, 2013).

Good, Timothy, *Above Top Secret: The Worldwide UFO Cover-up,* (Quill, 1989).

Gopnik, Alison, Andrew Meltzoff, and Patricia K. Kuhl, *The Scientist in the Crib*, (William Morrow, 2000).

Gore, Al, *An Inconvenient Truth: The Planetary Emergency of Global Warming and What We Can Do About It*, (Rodale Books, 2006).

Gould, Stephen Jay, *Time's Arrow, Time's Cycle: Myth and Metaphor in the Discovery of Geological Time*, (Harvard University Press, 1988).

Grant, Robert M., *Historical Introduction to the New Testament*, (Touchstone, 1972).

Grayling, A.C., *The GOD Argument: The Case Against Religion and for Humanism*, (Bloomsbury, 2014).

Gunther, John J., *Paul: Messenger and Exile,* (Judson Press, 1972).

Haidt, Jonathan, *The Righteous Mind: Why Good People Are Divided by Politics and Religion* (Vintage, 2013).

---, *The Happiness Hypothesis: Finding Modern Truth in Ancient Wisdom*, (Basic Books, 2006).

Hancock, Graham, *Fingerprints of the Gods*, (Three Rivers Press, 1996).

Harris, Sam, *The Moral Landscape: How Science Can Determine Human Values*, (Free Press, 2010).

Harrod, Ryan P., and Debra L. Martin, *Bioarchaeology of Cloimate Change and Violence: Ethical Considerations*, (Springer, 2013).

Hartman, William K., *Moons & Planets*, (BroksCole, 2004).

Haskins, Susan, *Mary Magdalene: Myth and Metaphor*, (Harcourt, 1994).

Hauser, Marc D., *Moral Minds: How Nature Designed Our Universal Sense of Right and Wrong*, (Ecco, 2006).

Hendel, Ronald S., "When the Sons of God Cavorted With the Daughters of Man," *Understanding the Dead Sea Scrolls,* Ed. Hershel Shanks, (Biblical Archaeology Society, 2012).

Hrdy, Sara Blaffer, *Mothers and Others: The Evolutionary Origins of Mutual Understanding*, (The Belknap Press, 2011).

James, William, *The Varieties of Religious Experience*, (CreateSpace, 2013).

Jastrow, Robert, *Journey to the Stars: Space Exploration—Tomorrow and Beyond*, (Bantam Books, 1989).

Jowett, George F., *The Drama of the Lost Disciples*, (Covenant Publishing, 2001).

Keltner, Dacher, *Born to Be Good: The Science of a Meaningful Life,* (W.W. Norton & Co., 2009).

Krauss, Lawrence M., *A Universe from Nothing: Why There is Something Rather Than Nothing,* (Atria, 2012).

Kung, Hans, *Judaism: Between Yesterday and Tomorrow,* (Crossroad, 1992).

Lerner, Eric J., *The Big Bang Never Happened: A Startling Refutation of the Dominant Theory of the Origin of the Universe,* (Vintage Books, 1992).

Lieberman, Daniel E., *The Evolution of the Human Head,* (Belnap Press, 2011).

Loeb, Abraham, *How Did the First Stars and Galaxies Form?,* (Princeton University Press, 2010).

Lovelock, James, *The Ages of Gaia: A Biography of Our Living Earth,* (W.W. Norton & Co., 1995).

Luhrmann, Tanya M., *When God Talks Back: Understanding the American Evangelical Relationship with God,* (Vintage, 2012).

Magnusson, Magnus, *The Archaeology of the Bible,* (Simon & Schuster, 1978).

Mann, Michael L., and Lee R. Kump, *Dire Predictions: Understanding Climate Change,* (DK, 2015).

Melton, Bruce, *Climate Discovery Chronicles: Recent, Relatively Unknown Discoveries About Our Rapidly Changing World,* (Amazon Digital Services, 2013).

Nowak, Martin, with Roger Highfield, *Super Cooperators: Altruism, Evolution, and Why We Need Each Other to Succeed*, (Free Press, 2012).

Paabo, Svante, *Neanderthal Man: In Search of Lost Genomes*, (Basic Books, 2015).

Pagels, Elaine, *The Gnostic Gospels*, (Vintage, 1989).

---, *Adam, Eve, and the Serpent: Sex and Politics in Early Christianity*, (Vintage, 1989).

Patrick, Sean, *Nikola Tesla: Imagination and the Man That Invented the 20th Century*, (Oculus, 2013).

Penrose, Roger, and Stuart Hameroff, *Consciousness and the Universe: Quantum Physics, Evolution, Brain & Mind,* (Cosmology Science Publishers, 2011).

Peters, Edward, *Inquisition*, (University of California Press, 1989).

Pfeiffer, Robert H., *History of the New Testament Times: With an Introduction to the Apocrypha,* (Forgotten Books, 2015).

Pickett, Kate, and Richard Wilkinson, *The Spirit Level: Why greater Equality Makes Societies Stronger*, (Bloomsbury Press, 2011).

Poole, Joyce, *Coming of Age with Elephants: A Memoir*, (Hyperior, 1996).

Prabhupada, A.C. Bhaktivedanta Swami, *Bhagavad-Gītā As It Is*, (Bhaktivedanta Book Trust, 1997).

Ridpath, Ian, *Messages from the Stars: Communication and Contact With Extraterrestrial Life*, (Harper & Row, 1978).

Robinson, James M., Ed., *The Nag Hammadi Library*, (Harper & Row, 1981).

Rudgley, Richard, *The Lost Civilizations of the Stone Age*, (Free Press, 2000).

Ryan, William & Pitman, Walter, *Noah's Flood: The New Scientific Discoveries About the Event That Changed History*, (Simon & Schuster, 2000).

Sagan, Carl, *The Dragons of Eden: Speculations on the Evolution of Human Intelligence*, (Ballantine Books, 1986).

Salzberg, Sharon, *Loving-Kindness: The Revolutionary Art of Happiness*, (Shambhala, 2002).

Sandel, Michael J., *Justice: What's the Right Thing to Do?*, (Farrar, Straus and Giroux, 2010).

Schaller, Mark, et al, Eds., *Evolution, Culture, and the Human Mind*, (Psychology Press, 2009).

Schonfield, Hugh Joseph, *The Passover Plot*, (Disinformation Books, 2004).

---, *The Jesus Party*, (Macmillan, 1974).

---, *Those Incredible Christians*, (Bantam Books, 1969).

---, *Secrets of the Dead Sea Scrolls*, (A.S. Barnes & Co., 1960).

Seung, Sebastian, *Connectome: How the Brain's Wiring Makes Us Who We Are*, (Houghton Mifflin Harcourt, 2012).

Sherosky, Frank J., *Millennial World Order: Discover the Spirit, Philosophy and Conditions of the Coming 1,000 Year Utopian Age*, (Strategic Publications, 1998).

Siegel, Daniel, *Mindsight: Transform Your Brain with the New Science of Kindness*, (Bantam, 2009).

Silberman, Neil Asher, *The Hidden Scrolls: Christianity, Judaism and the War for the Dead Sea Scrolls,* (G.P. Putnam's Sons, 1994).

Sobral, David, *Confessions of a Dark Energyholic, Old, Universe: Ours*, (Fitacita DS, 2012).

Stone, Merlin, *When God Was a Woman*, (Mariner Books, 1978).

Surowiecki, James, *The Wisdom of Crowds*, (Anchor, 2005).

Taylor, Jill Bolte, *My Stroke of Insight: A Brain Scientist's Personal Journey,* (Plume, 2009). (Of particular value in the chapter on Mind.)

Tilley, Lorna, *Theory and Practice in the Bioarchaeology of Care*, (Springer, 2015).

Tomasello, Michael, *Why We Cooperate*, (The MIT Press, 2009).

Tyson, Neil deGrasse, and Donald Goldsmith, *Origins: Fourteen Billion Years of Cosmic Evolution*, (W.W. Norton & Company, 2014).

Tyson, Neil deGrasse, *Space Chronicles: Facing the Ultimate Frontier*, (W.W. Norton & Company, 2013).

Vermes, Geza, *The Complete Dead Sea Scrolls in English*, (Penguin Classics, 2004).

Wilson, David Sloan, *Darwin's Cathedral: Evolution, Religion, and the Nature of Society*, (University of Chicago Press, 2003).

Winston, Patrick Henry, *Artificial Intelligence*, (Addison-Wesley Publishing Co., 1977).

Individuals

Professor Sushil Atreya, University of Michigan, Ann Arbor.

Dr. Bruno B. Averbeck, National Institute of Mental Health.

Professor Jeffrey Bada, University of California, San Diego.

Professor Rychard Bouwens, Leiden University.

Professor Peter R. Blake, Boston University.

Professor Kwabena Boahen, Stanford University.

Professor Dennis M. Bramble, University of Utah.

Professor Emeritus Thomas Dale Brock, University of Wisconsin, Madison.

Professor Randy L. Buckner, Harvard University.

Professor Jane E. Buikstra, Arizona State University.

Professor Chuansheng Chen, University of California, Irvine.

Professor Katherine Cronin, Max Planck Institute.

Professor Jozef Crutzen, Max Planck Institute for Chemistry.

Professor Carsten K.W. DeDreu, University of Amsterdam.

Professor Ana Duggan, Max Planck Institute.

Professor Laurent Excoffier, University of Bern.

Professor John Gatesy, University of California, Riverside.

Professor Katarina Gospic, Karolinska Institute in Stockholm.

Professor Garth Illingworth, University of California, Santa Cruz.

Professor Josephine Joordens, Leidens University.

Professor John T. Jost, New York University.

Professor Hillard S. Kaplan, University of New Mexico.

Professor Markus A. Keller, University of Cambridge.

Professor Kenneth B. Kidd, Yale University.

Professor Robert Knight, University of California, Berkeley.

Professor Fenna M. Krienen, George Washington University.

Professor Dan Magee, University of California, Santa Cruz.

Professor Shaun Marcott, University of Wisconsin-Madison.

Dr. Katherine McAuliffe, Yale University.

Dr. Dharmendra S. Modha, IBM Research, Cognitive Computing Group.

Professor Rachel Newcomb, Rollins College.

Professor James Noonan, Yale University.

Professor Diana Northrup, University of New Mexico.

Professor Maureen A. O'Leary, Stony Brook University on Long Island.

Dr. Pascal Oesch Yale University.

Professor John D. Polk, University of Illinois at Urbana-Champaign.

Professor David A. Raichlen, University of Arizona.

Professor Markus Ralser, University of Cambridge.

Professor James Rilling, Emory University.

Professor Bradley J. Ruffle, Ben Gurion University of Israel.

Professor Richard Sosis, University of Connecticut.

Professor Eugene F. Stoermer, University of Michigan.

Professor Alexandra V. Turchyn, University of Cambridge.

Professor Edwin van Leeuwen, Max Planck Institute.

Dr. William Tice Vicary, Los Angeles, California, M.D., J.D.

Dr. John R. Wible, Carnegie Museum of Natural History.

Professor Anne D. Yoder, Duke University.

WILLIAM JOHN COX

For more than 45 years, William John Cox has written extensively on law, politics, philosophy, and the human condition. During that time, he vigorously pursued  a career in law enforcement, public policy, and the law.

Cox was an early leader in the "New Breed" movement to professionalize law enforcement. He wrote the *Policy Manual* of the Los Angeles Police Department and the introductory chapters of the *Police Task Force Report* of the National Advisory Commission on Criminal Justice Standards and Goals, which continues to define the role of the police in America.

As an attorney, Cox worked for the U.S. Department of Justice to implement national standards and goals, prosecuted cases for the Los Angeles County District Attorney's Office, and operated a public interest law practice primarily dedicated to the defense of young people.

Cox volunteered *pro bono* services in several landmark legal cases. In 1979, he filed a class-action lawsuit on behalf of all citizens directly in the U.S. Supreme Court alleging that the government no longer represented the voters who elected it. As a remedy, Cox urged the Court to require national policy referendums to be held in conjunction with presidential elections.

In 1981, representing a Jewish survivor of Auschwitz, Cox investigated and successfully sued a group of radical right-wing organizations which denied the Holocaust. The case was the subject of the Turner Network Television motion picture, *Never Forget*.

Cox later represented a secret client and arranged the publication of almost 1,800 photographs of ancient manuscripts that had been kept from the public for more than 40 years. *A Facsimile Edition of the Dead Sea Scrolls* was published in November 1991.

He concluded his legal career as a Supervising Trial Counsel for the State Bar of California. There, Cox led a team of attorneys and investigators which prosecuted attorneys accused of serious misconduct and criminal gangs engaged in the illegal practice of law. He retired in 2007.

Continuing to concentrate on policy, political, and social issues since his retirement, Cox has lectured, taught classes at the university level, produced a series of articles and books, moderated several Internet websites, and maintained an extensive worldwide correspondence. He can be contacted through his website at www.williamjohncox.com.

Made in the USA
Middletown, DE
05 January 2023

21495340R00070